COUNTRIES OF THE WORLD

PORTUGAL

Joy Gregory

AV2

www.openlightbox.com

AV2

Step 1
Go to **www.openlightbox.com**

Step 2
Enter this unique code
XGNCLYAF4

Step 3
Explore your interactive eBook!

AV2 is optimized for use on any device

Your interactive eBook comes with...

Contents
Browse a live contents page to easily navigate through resources

Audio
Listen to sections of the book read aloud

Videos
Watch informative video clips

Weblinks
Gain additional information for research

Slideshows
View images and captions

Try This!
Complete activities and hands-on experiments

Key Words
Study vocabulary, and complete a matching word activity

Quizzes
Test your knowledge

Share
Share titles within your Learning Management System (LMS) or Library Circulation System

Citation
Create bibliographical references following APA, CMOS, and MLA styles

This title is part of our AV2 digital subscription

1-Year 3–8 Subscription
ISBN 978-1-7911-3306-1

Access hundreds of AV2 titles with our digital subscription.
Sign up for a FREE trial at **www.openlightbox.com/trial**

The digital components of this book are guaranteed to stay active for at least five years from the date of publication.

Portugal

CONTENTS

Portugal Overview

Portugal is one of the oldest countries in Europe. Founded in 1143, it was governed as a **monarchy** for more than 750 years. Portugal was the world's first global **empire**. It controlled **colonies** in Africa and Asia, and ruled all of Brazil as well. This put Portugal at the center of the global sea trade at the time. Its ships supplied Europe with goods from its colonies and other exotic locations. All of this brought great wealth to the country. Today, Portugal is officially known as the Portuguese **Republic**. The country is renowned for its sunny days, sandy beaches, and terraced vineyards.

Portuguese couple in traditional clothing

Portugal experiences more than **300 days of sunshine** every year.

In **2022**, Portugal was ranked the world's **6th most peaceful nation**, after Iceland, New Zealand, Ireland, Denmark, and Austria.

Portugal is home to the world's **oldest bookstore**. Called Bertrand, it opened in **1732**.

The Douro River winds its way through one of the oldest wine-producing regions on Earth.

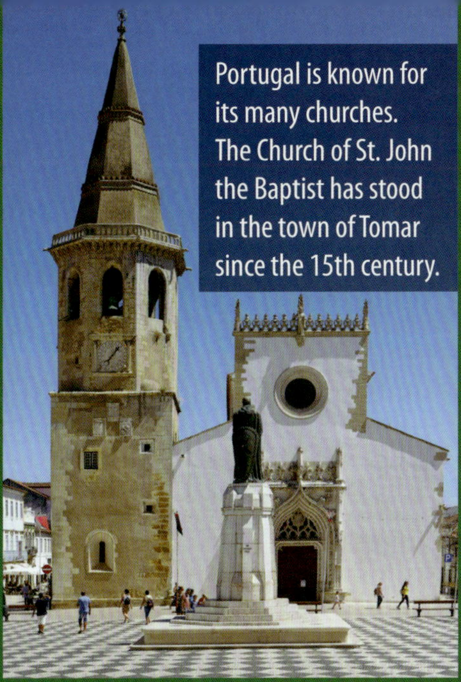

Portugal is known for its many churches. The Church of St. John the Baptist has stood in the town of Tomar since the 15th century.

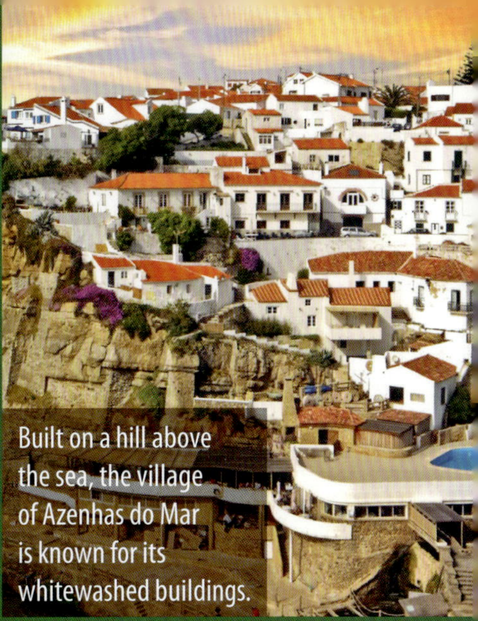

Built on a hill above the sea, the village of Azenhas do Mar is known for its whitewashed buildings.

Portugal is home to about 200 Iberian lynx, currently considered to be the one of the world's most endangered cats.

Seafood , including octopus, forms the basis of some of Portugal's most popular dishes.

Located on the southern coast, Benagil Cathedral is a large cave created by ocean waves. Small boats take people inside the cave, which has a huge eye-shaped hole.

The glass skywalk at Cabo Girão, Madeira, offers spectacular views of the ocean coast and nearby cities. The skywalk is 1,903 feet (580 meters) above sea level.

Exploring Portugal

Portugal is located on the west side of the Iberian **Peninsula**. Covering 35,608 square miles (92,224 square kilometers) of land, the country is 349 miles (562 kilometers) long and 135 miles (217 km) wide. To the west and south, Portugal borders the Atlantic Ocean. The rest of the country shares a border with Spain. The Portuguese Republic includes two archipelagos, or groups of islands. Both archipelagos are far away from mainland Portugal. The Azores islands are about 1,000 miles (1,609 km) from Portugal's west coast, while the islands in the Madeira group are 600 miles (966 km) away from the mainland.

A Serra da Estrela

The Serra da Estrela range includes the highest mountains on mainland Portugal. The range is situated between the Mondego and Tagus Rivers. It stretches 40 miles (65 km) from the northeast to southwest and is 10 to 15 miles (16 to 24 km) wide.

B Mondego River

The Mondego River is the longest river that begins and ends in Portugal. It runs 161 miles (259 km) from the Serra da Estrela to the Atlantic Ocean. Several dams have been built along the river to aid in the production of **hydroelectricity** for the country.

C Lisbon

Lisbon is Portugal's capital and largest city. Located on the Tagus River, it is about 8 miles (13 km) from the Atlantic Ocean. This has made the city a major shipping hub. With a metropolitan area covering 370 square miles (958 sq. km), Lisbon is home to approximately 3 million people.

D Alqueva Reservoir

The Alqueva Reservoir is one of the largest artificial lakes in Europe. Built on the Guadiana River, the reservoir covers 97 square miles (251 sq. km) of land in southern Portugal. It provides hydroelectricity and a secure source of water for both people and farms.

Map of Portugal

Land and Climate

Tagus River

Despite its relatively small size, mainland Portugal has a diverse range of landscapes. These include mountains, vast plains, and a variety of coastal features. The landforms change from north to south.

Mountains and forested valleys are mostly located in the area north of the Tagus River. Central and southern Portugal have low-lying plains. Much of this land includes **fertile** soil, while some areas feature rugged **plateaus** of exposed rock. The western coast of Portugal has sandy beaches and rocky cliffs.

Mount Pico Is Portugal's highest mountain. Located in the Azores, Pico is a stratovolcano that has been dormant, or inactive, for more than 300 years.

Portugal's Tallest Mountains

Mount Pico
The Azores
1

7,713 feet (2,351 m)

Torre
Serra da Estrala
2

6,539 feet (1,993 m)

Pico Ruivo
Madeira Islands
3

6,106 feet (1,861 m)

Portugal has very few natural lakes. However, reservoirs were built on most of the country's main rivers. Their water is used for human consumption, recreation, and irrigation. Similar to the Alqueva Reservoir, some of these man-made lakes are used to generate electric power.

Lagoa do Fogo, a crater lake in the Azores

Both the Azores and Madeira archipelagos were formed by volcanic activity. Their islands feature coastlines with rocky shores and rugged sea cliffs. Lush forests make up their interiors. Vast craters indicate where volcanoes once were. Some have filled with water and are now turquoise-blue lakes. Hot springs and thermal pools are common.

Mainland Portugal has a temperate climate, meaning that it has moderate temperatures year-round. During the winter months, the average daytime temperature reaches 61° Fahrenheit (16° Celsius). By May, the daytime average temperature rises to 72°F (22°C). July and August are Portugal's hottest summer months, with daytime temperatures averaging about 78°F (26°C). Very little rain falls during the summer months. When rain does arrive, it tends to affect the north more than the south. The northern city of Braga records 57 inches (1,448 millimeters) of rain a year on average. Algarve, in the south, receives only 20 inches (508 mm). The Azores and Madeira have climates similar to the mainland.

Portugal's mainland coast stretches along 528 miles (850 km) of terrain.

Plants and Animals

Cork oak

A variety of plants and animals can be found in Portugal. Plant life differs from region to region. Birch, chestnut, and maple trees grow in the north. Eucalyptus and olive trees are more common in central Portugal. The south is known for its maritime pine and cork oak. These **species** can grow in the drier conditions found there. Herbs such as lavender and thyme are some of the smaller plants that grow in Portugal.

Portugal's natural areas provide good **habitat** for many animals. Rabbit, fox, and the Iberian hare are found throughout the country. Deer, wild goats, and pigs are also common. Wolves are rare. Some live in remote parts of the north and northeast. The Malcata Nature Reserve in central Portugal was created to protect the Iberian lynx.

Both Madeira and the Azores are known for their flowering plants. Game birds, such as quail and red partridge, are common to Azores. About 40 species of birds breed on the Madeira islands. Madeira also has more than 100 species of moths. The Mediterranean monk seal is **native** to Madeira. That species of seal is endangered.

The Mediterranean monk seal is one of the world's rarest marine mammals. It is estimated that there are only 600 to 700 of these seals left in the world.

Natural Resources

Fish and forests are two of Portugal's most important natural resources. About 70 species of fish live in the country's waters. Hake, sardines, and mackerel are common. Some fishers make their living catching octopus.

Fishers with sardine catch

Close to one-third of the world's cork oak trees grow in Portugal. The bark of these trees is harvested to make products such as shoes, bags, and flooring. Cork oaks can be stripped of their bark every 9 to 12 years. This process does not harm the trees.

Portugal's fertile soil is another important natural resource. It allows for a variety of crops to be grown in the country. Common crops include wheat, barley, corn, and grapes. Some farmers grow potatoes, olives, and tomatoes.

Portugal uses the wind, sunlight, and water to make electricity. These natural resources are **renewable**. By 2026, more than 80 percent of Portugal's electricity will be produced by renewables. They will replace electricity made by burning fossil fuels. Fossil fuels, such as coal and oil, pollute the air. They also speed up **climate change**.

Vineyards cover approximately 480,000 acres (194,249 hectares) of Portugal's terrain. The grapes grown in the country are used to make a wide variety of wines.

Tourism

Surfing at Nazare's North Beach

Portugal is a very popular tourist destination. More than 15 million tourists visited the country in 2022 alone. The tourism industry adds in excess of $40 billion a year to Portugal's **economy**. Many people come to Portugal to experience its warm winters, sunny beaches, and good food.

Surfing enthusiasts are common visitors to Portugal. They come to an area called the Silver Coast, located between Porto and Lisbon. The Silver Coast includes two beaches that attract experienced surfers from all over the world. Supertubos Beach is by Peniche. North Beach is near Nazaré. This beach is known for having the world's largest waves. Some can reach heights of 115 feet (35 m) or more.

Pena National Palace was built in the 19th century on the site of a former monastery.

Pena National Palace receives between **18 and 20 million** visitors annually.

On a clear day, Pena National Palace can be seen all the way from Lisbon, some **31 miles (50 km)** away.

The park surrounding the palace covers an area of **210 acres (85 ha)**.

Portugal has several parks and wildlife reserves for fans of the outdoors. Hikers often head to Serra da Estrela Natural Park to explore its 233 miles (375 km) of marked trails. Birdwatchers arrive hoping to spot the eagles, owls, and buzzards that soar above. Madeira Natural Park covers two-thirds of Madeira Island, protecting its fragile ecosystems. Visitors to the park can walk through forests relatively untouched by human development and view a variety of endangered plants and animals.

Madeira Natural Park

Portugal's many historical sites also draw travelers to the country. Lisbon's Belem Tower was built in 1515 to defend the city from invaders. The colorful Pena National Palace, in Sintra, was once the summer home for Portugal's royal family. The prehistoric rock art sites in the Côa Valley are also popular places to visit.

Important religious sites can be found throughout Portugal. These sites attract both tourists and **pilgrims**. The Bom Jesus do Monte is a large sanctuary near Braga. It features numerous chapels, statues, and fountains, as well as a grand staircase. The Jerónimos Monastery, in Lisbon, was built in the 16th century to serve as a monument to Portuguese explorer Vasco da Gama.

The Monument to the Discoveries, near Lisbon, marks the death of Henry the Navigator. This member of the Portuguese royal family sponsored numerous explorations in the Atlantic Ocean, resulting in the discovery of the Azores and Madeira in the 1400s.

Industry

Tourism is Portugal's biggest industry, employing about 380,000 of the country's residents. The majority of these people work in restaurants, hotels, and transportation services. In 2022, about 79,000 companies in Portugal were linked to the travel business.

Manufacturing is another key industry. Portugal is home to several vehicle production plants. Automobiles are one of the country's biggest **exports**. Other companies make tools and medicines. Portugal also produces **textiles**, shoes, and clothing. Some manufacturers make cork into wine bottle stoppers. This is one of the main uses of cork grown in Portugal.

Food production is an important contributor to Portugal's economy. In 2020, the country grew about 1.4 million tons (1.27 million metric tons) of tomatoes, most of which were sold to companies that make tomato paste. Portugal is one of the world's largest exporters of this product. Portuguese farmers grow more than 250 kinds of grapes. Most of these grapes are used to make wine. Today, Portugal ranks as the world's ninth-largest exporter of wine. The country is also known for its canned sardines.

Portugal exported $9.7 billion of automobiles in 2022, accounting for 11.8 percent of Portugal's total exports for the year.

Goods and Services

Portugal produces goods that are in demand around the world. In fact, in 2022, the country exported more than $82 billion worth of goods worldwide. However, Portugal's most important trade relations are with other European countries. Not only does Portugal export its products to these countries, it also **imports** products from them.

Hotel concierge, Lisbon

Spain is Portugal's closest neighbor and biggest trading partner. It buys approximately one quarter of the goods Portugal exports. That includes 35 percent of Portugal's fruit, vegetable, and flower exports. In turn, Portugal imports about $33 billion of goods from Spain every year. The top products imported from Spain are mineral fuels, automobile parts, and electrical equipment. Portugal's next-largest trading partners are France, Germany, and the United States.

In Portugal, most jobs are in the service industry. People in this industry do not create goods. Instead, they provide assistance and knowledge to consumers. Portugal's services sector includes jobs in tourism, banking, healthcare, education, and **telecommunications**.

Many of the goods shipped to and from Portugal transit through the Port of Lisbon, the country's main seaport. The port handles approximately 13.2 million tons (11.8 million metric tons) of cargo per year.

Ancient Peoples

Viriathus, warrior who led Lusitanians during the Roman invasion

Humans have lived in Portugal for more than 100,000 years. These first peoples are believed to have survived by hunting and fishing. By about 5000 BC, people had begun to farm the land. Early farmers settled in the Tagus River valley, where they could use the river water to irrigate crops. Over time, these settlers formed a society with its own customs and traditions. They became known as the Iberians.

In about 700 BC, **Celtic** tribes arrived from the north and settled in what are now north and west Portugal. They eventually intermarried with the local people. Some of them settled in central Portugal. These people became known as the Lusitanians. The Lusitanians developed their own language and customs. They are considered the ancestors of modern-day Portuguese.

Remains of the Roman occupation can still be seen in parts of Portugal. The Roman temple in Evora has stood in the town center since the 1st century AD.

Other groups, including the Phoenicians and Greeks, also moved into what is now Portugal, settling in the south and along the coast. However, in about 200 BC, the Romans took control of the Iberian Peninsula. They were in charge of the region until the 4th century. Over the next 800 years, Portugal was invaded several times. The invaders came from other parts of Europe as well as Africa.

The Age of Exploration

An independent country since the 1140s, Portugal had pushed its final invaders off its land by the middle of the 13th century. Over the next 200 years, Portugal developed a shipbuilding industry. Its sailors learned how to navigate the ocean. Early voyages saw them explore islands off the northwest coast of Africa. Portuguese ships brought foreign goods, including spices and gold, back to Portugal for sale. With time, Portugal become a major shipping hub.

In 1488, Portuguese ships sailed around the southern tip of Africa. Another Portuguese ship reached India in 1498. A few years later, the Portuguese landed in Japan. These trips opened new trade routes. Goods from Africa, India, and Asia were sold to markets in Europe. In the 1530s, Portugal colonized Brazil. Soon, Brazil was the world's biggest exporter of sugar, tobacco, and diamonds.

It was not long before Portugal had colonies in several parts of the world. Portugal not only claimed ownership of the resources in these colonies, but the people as well. In Africa specifically, slaves were forced to work in sugar cane fields. The sugar they produced was shipped to Portugal for sale. Other slaves were sold to people in the Americas. Slaves continued to be used in Portuguese colonies until 1869.

Portuguese sailors often traveled on caravels during the Age of Exploration. Reproductions of these small ships allow tourists to learn more about Portugal's seafaring past.

Conflict and Resolution

King Manuel II was the last king of Portugal. He reigned from 1908 to 1910.

In its early days, Portugal was ruled by a series of monarchs. Between 1580 and 1668, the country was under the control of the Spanish monarchy. In 1668, Spain gave Portugal its independence. A new Portuguese king, Peter II, became the ruler. He was able to use the discovery of gold in Brazil to build Portuguese wealth.

By the late 19th century, many Portuguese were unhappy with the royal family. They wanted more say in how Portugal was governed. They called for Portugal to have a **democratic** form of government. In 1910, there was a revolution. The Portuguese monarch lost his power. Portugal adopted a new **constitution**. Its laws included rules for elections, allowing some adult males to vote.

On the day of the Carnation Revolution, people flooded into the streets to show their support for the soldiers staging the takeover.

Most of Portugal's first political leaders were autocratic. This meant they had absolute control over how the country was run. Portugal suffered under this form of leadership. Politicians took money that was supposed to help people. They gave well-paying jobs to their friends. The economy faltered. Portugal's citizens saw what was happening. They held protests for change.

In 1926, Portugal fell victim to a military **coup**. The country became a **dictatorship**, initially controlled by a series of military leaders. In 1932, a politician named Antonio Salazar became prime minister. He drew up a new constitution for the country. It banned political parties and allowed only those who supported the government to take office. Salazar led Portugal for more than 30 years.

On April 25, 1974, Portugal experienced another military coup. Called the Carnation Revolution, it resulted in the country becoming a democracy. April 25 is now a national holiday in Portugal. It is called Freedom Day.

Over the years, Portugal had faced international pressure to dissolve its colonial empire. The country had given Brazil its independence in 1822, but had refused to give up control of its colonies in Africa and Asia. It was only in 1975 that the empire began to be dismantled. That year, Portugal granted freedom to its African colonies, Angola and Mozambique. In 1999, the last vestiges of the Portuguese Empire came to an end when Portugal returned the control of Macau to China.

A formal ceremony marked the return of Macau to China. The Portuguese flag was lowered for the last time and given to Macau's governor, Rocha Vieira.

Population

More than 10.2 million people live in Portugal. About 67 percent of them live in **urban** areas. Most people live in towns and cities along the coast. The two largest cities are Lisbon and Porto. Lisbon has 3 million residents, while 1.3 million people live in Porto.

Portugal has a young population, with 65 percent of its residents between 15 and 64 years old. Those over 65 make up 23 percent of the country's population. The total number of residents is falling. People are not having as many children as they used to, and many of Portugal's young people are moving to other countries for better employment opportunities. To maintain its population, Portugal needs people to move there from other places. The country is currently developing programs to encourage **immigration**.

Almost 96 percent of the population over the age of 15 can read and write. Children aged 6 to 18 must attend school. Most Portuguese students attend public schools located near their homes. All students are required to study English.

The city of Porto

Politics and Government

Portugal is a semi-presidential republic. This means that it has an elected government that is led by a president and a prime minister. Every four years, voters in Portugal elect their parliament. The parliament is responsible for making the country's laws. Those laws are enforced by the judiciary, another branch of government.

Portugal's parliament is made up of 230 members. Four of them are elected by citizens who live abroad. However, none of the members serve a particular region. Instead, they serve the country at large. Most members of the parliament belong to a political party. The leader of the party that won the election usually becomes prime minister and leads the parliament.

Portugal elects a president every five years. The president is the country's head of state. He or she represents the country both at home and internationally. While this role is largely ceremonial, Portugal's president is responsible for calling elections and formally appointing a prime minister to run the parliament. He or she is also in charge of the country's military.

António Luís Santos da Costa, Portugal's 119th prime minister

The Portuguese parliament building in Lisbon was built in the 16th century. It used to be a Benedictine monastery.

Cultural Groups

While some countries are made up of people from many different backgrounds, Portugal is less culturally diverse. The majority of people living in Portugal were born there. They come from families that have lived in the country since ancient times.

The Roma have a more recent history in the country. They began arriving in Portugal in the late 15th century from Spain. Today, approximately 40,000 Portuguese citizens are Roma. Most live in the Algarve area, in southern Portugal. They tend to live close to each other. This helps them maintain their culture. Many Roma sell handicrafts and clothing at markets in **rural** areas.

In recent years, more people from other cultures have begun moving to Portugal. Some of them come from places that used to be Portuguese colonies, such as Brazil. Others come from different countries in Africa and Asia. Most newcomers settle in Lisbon.

People with **Portuguese ancestry** make up about **95 percent** of Portugal's population.

Close to **100 percent** of the people who live in Portugal speak **Portuguese** as their first language.

Approximately **80 percent** of Portugal's population is **Roman Catholic**.

Street markets have been part of Portuguese culture for centuries. At modern markets, locals and tourists pick up farm-fresh produce, clothes, and souvenirs.

Almost every person living in Portugal speaks Portuguese, one of the country's two official languages. The second official language is Mirandese. This language is mainly spoken in an area known as Miranda do Duoro, which is located in northeastern Portugal, along the Spanish border. About 5,000 people in the area speak Mirandese on a regular basis. Another 10,000 speak the language now and then.

Paulitieros dancers from Miranda do Douro

Religion plays a major role in Portugal's cultural landscape. Most people living in Portugal are Roman Catholic. Many of the country's main festivals and celebrations coincide with the Catholic religious calendar. Some of the biggest festivals are at Christmas and Easter. Others honor the lives of special saints. These events give families and neighbors a reason to gather.

When people come together, they often eat foods that are part of their cultural tradition. Most meals begin with soup and bread. The main meal may include popular Portuguese dishes such as pork sausage or fresh seafood. The country is famous for its sweet wines. These are served before or after a meal.

Every four years since the 14th century, the citizens of Tomar have held a religious festival known as the *Festa dos Tabuleiros*, or Festival of the Trays. The main event is a parade that features young women wearing crowns adorned with colored paper flowers and bread.

Arts and Entertainment

Vasco Fernandes was known for his paintings of religious scenes.

Portugal is known for *fado*, its traditional form of music. Originating in Lisbon in the early 19th century, fado songs are often melancholic and tell stories about life's challenges. They are played at cafes and community gatherings. Fado singers are usually accompanied by guitars and violins.

The Portuguese are also known for their art. The Grão Vasco National Museum, in the city of Viseu, exhibits Portuguese paintings from the 15th century. The museum is named after a painter named Vasco Fernandes. He was nicknamed *Grão Vasco*, which means Vasco the Great. The Paula Rego House of Stories, in Cascais, is a museum devoted to the work of its namesake. Paula Rego was known internationally for painting scenes of Portuguese life and culture.

Lisbon is also home to several art museums. The National Museum of Ancient Art's collection is a showcase for works from the 12th to 19th centuries. The National Contemporary Art Museum is a showcase for more modern works.

The National Azulejo Museum in Lisbon showcases a special kind of Portuguese art. Azulejos are blue and white painted tiles. Since the 14th century, they have been used to decorate Portuguese buildings. Some of the tiles tell stories about life in Portugal. Azulejos are also found in many churches and public areas.

The National Azulejo Museum in Lisbon

Portugal has a small but active film industry. It produces about 10 films a year, most of which are for the local market. The theater scene also focuses on producing works for its home audience. A style of play called *Revista* is popular in the country. Revistas are comedic plays that use **satire** to get their point across. They were developed in Portugal in the 20th century. Plays of all kinds can be seen at the annual Almada Theatre Festival. In operation for more than 40 years, this festival is a cooperative venture between the cities of Almada and Lisbon. It features not only plays from Portugal, but from around the world as well.

Daniela Ruah plays Kensi in *NCIS: Los Angeles.* Born in the United States, she grew up in Portugal. It is there that her acting career began.

Sports

Cristiano Ronaldo

Portugal is a soccer country. People play it recreationally and attend professional games in droves. The country has three top-rated professional soccer teams. Sporting CP and S.L. Benfica are based in Lisbon, while Porto FC plays out of its namesake city. Most Portuguese have a favorite team. They also cheer for local clubs. The sport is so popular that even local games are broadcast on live television.

Cristiano Ronaldo is one of the world's best-known soccer players. Born in Madeira, he went on to play professionally for clubs in England, Spain, and Italy. In 2022, he signed with a club in Saudi Arabia. Ronaldo played for Portugal at five **World Cup** tournaments. In international matches, he has scored more goals than any other men's player in the world.

In 2019, Portugal's national soccer team won the Nations League title. Their final score against the Netherlands was 1–0.

During her 15 years with the WNBA, Ticha Penicheiro was a four-time WNBA All-Star. She helped lead the Sacramento Monarchs to the championship title in 2005.

Basketball is also popular in Portugal. The country's top teams often compete in European championships. In 2021, the National Basketball Association (NBA) in America drafted its first Portuguese player. His name is Neemias Queta. In 2023, Queta played for the Boston Celtics. Ticha Penicheiro is also from Portugal. She played in the Women's National Basketball Association (WNBA). In 2019, Penicheiro was inducted into the Women's Basketball Hall of Fame. For most of her career, she played point guard for the Sacramento Monarchs.

Portugal is the location of one of the world's premier cycling events. Thousands of people from all over the world watch the Tour of Portugal. Held over a two-week period, this race attracts the world's top cycling teams. The first Tour of Portugal was held in 1927.

Campo Pequeno bullring, Lisbon

Bullfighting has been a cultural tradition in Portugal for hundreds of years. The fights are held in special arenas. They feature bullfighters called *cavaleiros* who challenge the bull while riding a horse. Unlike some forms of bullfighting, Portuguese bullfighters do not try to kill the bull.

Activity

Mapping Portugal

We use many tools to interpret maps and to understand the locations of features such as cities, states, lakes, and rivers. The map on the following page has many tools to help interpret information on the map of Portugal.

Mapping Tools

The compass rose shows north, south, east, and west. The points in between represent northeast, northwest, southeast, and southwest.

The map scale shows that the distances on a map represent much longer distances in real life. If you measure the distance between objects on a map, you can use the map scale to calculate the actual distance in miles or kilometers between those two points.

The lines of latitude and longitude are long lines that appear on maps. The lines of latitude run east to west and measure how far north or south of the equator a place is located. The lines of longitude run north to south and measure how far east or west of the Prime Meridian a place is located. A location on a map can be found by using the two numbers where latitude and longitude meet. This number is called a coordinate and is written using degrees and direction. For example, the city of Lisbon would be found at 38°N and 9°W on a map.

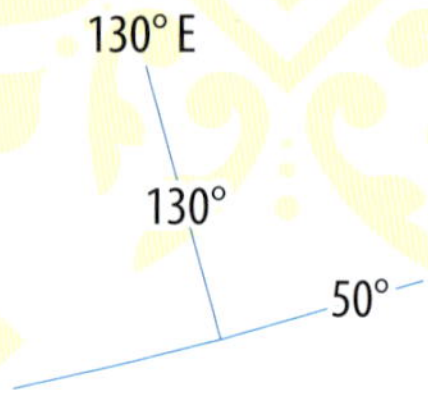

MAP IT!

Using the map and the appropriate tools, complete the activities below.

Locating with latitude and longitude

1. Which city is found at 41°N and 8°W?
2. Which town is found at 38°N and 7°W?
3. Which mountain peak is found at 40°N and 7°W?

Distances between points

4. Using the map scale and a ruler, calculate the approximate distance between the cities of Lisbon and the fishing village of Peniche.
5. Using the map scale and a ruler, calculate how long Portugal's section of the Tagus River is, including the part it shares with the Spanish border.
6. Using the map scale and a ruler, calculate the approximate distance between Porto and Faro.

ANSWERS 1. Porto 2. Evora 3. Torre 4. 60 miles (97 km) 5. 138 miles (222 km) 6. 344 miles (554 km)

Map of Portugal

Legend

Capital City
City
Water
Rivers
Country Border
Mountains
Longitude & Latitude
Portugal
Other Countries

SCALE 50 kilometers 50 miles

Quiz

1 Which archipelagos are part of Portugal?

2 What is the capital of Portugal?

3 What is the population of Portugal?

4 Where was soccer star Cristiano Ronaldo born?

5 What is the name of the peninsula on which Portugal is located?

6 How many members make up Portugal's parliament?

7 When did the Roma first begin arriving in Portugal?

8 What type of Portuguese music is known for its melancholic style?

ANSWERS
1. The Azores and Madeira **2.** Lisbon **3.** More than 10.2 million **4.** Madeira **5.** Iberian Peninsula **6.** 230 **7.** Late 15th century **8.** Fado

Key Words

Celtic: referring to the culture of an ancient European people who are related to the Irish, Scots, Welsh, and Bretons

climate change: long-term shifts in temperatures and weather patterns

colonies: areas or countries that are under the control of another country

constitution: a written document stating a country's basic principles and laws

coup: the sudden, violent overthrow of an existing government

democratic: a type of government in which people choose their leaders by voting

dictatorship: a country that is ruled by a very strict and harsh government

economy: the wealth and resources of a country or area

empire: a group of countries ruled by a single person, government, or country

exports: products sold to another country

fertile: able to produce many crops

habitat: a place where a plant, animal, or other organism makes its home

hydroelectricity: power produced using the energy of moving water

immigration: the movement of people to a new country or area

imports: buys goods from another country

monarchy: a form of government led by a king or queen

native: from a particular place

peninsula: an area of land surrounded on three sides by water

pilgrims: people who journey to a sacred place for religious reasons

plateaus: flat pieces of land that rise sharply above surrounding land

renewable: able to be replaced

republic: a form of government in which the head of state is elected

rural: relating to the countryside

satire: the use of humor and sarcasm to make a point or expose a truth

species: organisms that share common characteristics

telecommunications: technologies, such as radios, televisions, or phones, that allow the sharing of information over large distances

textiles: woven or knit fabrics

urban: relating to a city or town

World Cup: a soccer tournament held every four years to determine a world champion

Index

Get the best of both worlds.

AV2 bridges the gap between print and digital.

The expandable resources toolbar enables quick access to content including **videos**, **audio**, **activities**, **weblinks**, **slideshows**, **quizzes**, and **key words**.

Animated videos make static images come alive.

Resource icons on each page help readers to further **explore key concepts**.

Published by Lightbox Learning Inc.
276 5th Avenue, Suite 704 #917
New York, NY 10001
Website: www.openlightbox.com

Library of Congress Cataloging-in-Publication data available upon request.

ISBN 979-8-8745-0373-4 (hardcover)
ISBN 979-8-8745-0374-1 (softcover)
ISBN 979-8-8745-0375-8 (static multi-user eBook)
ISBN 979-8-8745-0377-2 (interactive multi-user eBook)

Printed in Guangzhou, China
1 2 3 4 5 6 7 8 9 0 27 26 25 24 23

122023
101323

Project Coordinator: Heather Kissock
Designer: Terry Paulhus
Layout: Mandy Christiansen

Photo Credits
Every reasonable effort has been made to trace ownership and to obtain permission to reprint copyright material. The publisher would be pleased to have any errors or omissions brought to its attention so that they may be corrected in subsequent printings. The publisher acknowledges Getty Images, Alamy, Shutterstock, Newscom, and Wikimedia Commons as its primary image suppliers for this title.